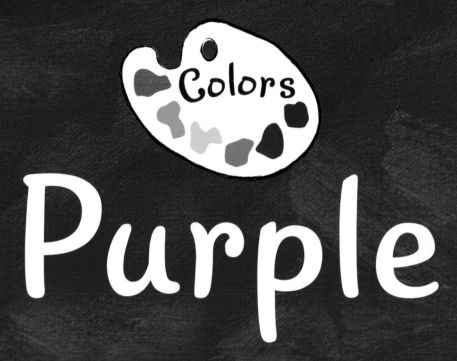

Colors

Purple

by Sarah L. Schuette

Reading Consultant:
Elena Bodrova, Ph.D., Senior Consultant,
Mid-continent Research for Education and Learning

an imprint of Capstone Press
Mankato, Minnesota

A+ Books are published by Capstone Press
151 Good Counsel Drive, P.O. Box 669, Mankato, Minnesota 56002
http://www.capstone-press.com

1 2 3 4 5 6 07 06 05 04 03 02

Library of Congress Cataloging-in-Publication Data
Schuette, Sarah L., 1976–
 Purple / by Sarah L. Schuette.
 p. cm.—(Colors)
 Summary: Text and photographs describe common things that are purple, including eggplants, grape jelly, and flowers.
 Includes bibliographical references and index.
 ISBN 0-7368-1470-1 (hardcover)
 1. Purple—Juvenile literature. [1. Purple] I. Title.
QC495.5 .S366 2003
535.6—dc21   2002000704

Created by the A+ Team
Sarah L. Schuette, editor; Heather Kindseth, production designer; Patrick D. Dentinger, production designer; Gary Sundermeyer, photographer; Nancy White, photo stylist

A+ Books thanks Michael Dahl for editorial assistance.

Note to Parents, Teachers, and Librarians

The Colors series uses full-color photographs and a nonfiction format to introduce children to the world of color. *Purple* is designed to be read aloud to a pre-reader or to be read independently by an early reader. Photographs and activities help early readers and listeners understand the text and concepts discussed. The book encourages further learning by including the following sections: Table of Contents, Words to Know, Read More, Internet Sites, and Index. Early readers may need assistance using these features.

Table of Contents

Purple blooms and
purple flowers.

Rain helps flowers grow. The iris is a flower with purple petals. The tall flowers bloom every year.

6

Purple grows tall
from spring showers.

Purple cabbage grows well in cool weather. This vegetable tastes good in salads.

Purple is leafy.
Purple is round.

Plums are purple fruits. They grow on trees. Dried plums turn into prunes.

Purple can grow
above the ground.

Purple ripens on a warm, sunny day.

An eggplant can grow as large as a football. Most people think that an eggplant is a vegetable. It is really a fruit.

You can toss a boomerang in the air. It will come back to you.

14

Purple comes back from flying far away.

Purple spreads on a piece of bread.

People add sugar
to grape juice.
They cook the juice
to make jelly.

Hats are important.
A hat warms your head
on cold, windy days.

Purple sits high on
top of your head.

Purple cloth used to cost a lot of money. Only queens and kings had enough money to buy purple cloth.

Purple is worn by queens and kings.

Crayons are sticks of colored wax. Other names for purple crayons are lilac and plum.

Purple can make more purple things.

Purple is sweet.
Purple is chilly.

Grapes grow on vines. People squeeze grapes to make juice. Grape juice tastes sweet.

Purple is fun.
Purple is silly!

Making Purple

Artists use a color wheel to know how to mix colors. Yellow, red, and blue are primary colors. They mix together to make secondary colors. Purple, orange, and green are the secondary colors they make. You can make purple by mixing blue and red.

You will need

2 small cartons of vanilla yogurt

2 bowls

blue and red food coloring

2 spoons

graham crackers

color wheel

1 Pour one carton of yogurt into a bowl. Add four drops of blue food coloring. Stir with a spoon until the yogurt is dyed blue.

2 Pour the other carton of yogurt into the second bowl. Add eight drops of red food coloring. Stir with a spoon until the yogurt is dyed red. The yogurt may look pink. Pink is a tint of red. Adding white to a color makes a tint.

3 Wash your hands and dip into the bowls with your fingers. Mix the red and blue yogurt together on a graham cracker. What color does it make? See what designs you can make on the cracker. You can eat the cracker and yogurt for a snack.

Words to Know

fruit—the fleshy, juicy part of a plant that people eat; plums, grapes, and eggplants are purple fruits.

king—a man from a royal family who is the ruler of a country

petal—one of the colored outer parts of a flower

queen—a woman from a royal family who is the ruler of a country

vegetable—a plant grown for food; cabbage is a purple vegetable.

vine—a plant with a long stem that grows along the ground; grapes grow on woody vines.

wax—a substance made from fat or oil that is used to make crayons; crayons are many colors.

Read More

Rau, Dana Meachen. *Purple Is Best.* A Rookie Reader. New York: Children's Press, 1999.

Salzmann, Mary Elizabeth. *Purple.* What Color Is It? Edina, Minn.: Abdo, 1999.

Internet Sites

I Love Colors—Purple Things
http://www.enchantedlearning.com/colors/purple.shtml

Purple Paint Bear
http://www.thelittleartist.com/purple.html

Index